INDIANA

EXPLORE THE UNITED STATES ★ EXPLORE THE UNITED STATES ★ EXPLORE THE UNITED STATES ★ EXPLORE THE UNITED STATES

Julie Murray

Big Buddy BOOKS
Explore the United States

VISIT US AT

www.abdopublishing.com

Published by ABDO Publishing Company, PO Box 398166, Minneapolis, MN 55439.

Copyright © 2013 by Abdo Consulting Group, Inc. International copyrights reserved in all countries. No part of this book may be reproduced in any form without written permission from the publisher. Big Buddy Books™ is a trademark and logo of ABDO Publishing Company.

Printed in the United States of America, North Mankato, Minnesota.
032012
092012

PRINTED ON RECYCLED PAPER

Coordinating Series Editor: Rochelle Baltzer
Editor: Sarah Tieck
Contributing Editors: Megan M. Gunderson, BreAnn Rumsch, Marcia Zappa
Graphic Design: Adam Craven
Cover Photograph: *Shutterstock*: Kenneth Keifer.
Interior Photographs/Illustrations: *Alamy*: Dennis MacDonald (p. 11); *AP Photo*: Cal Sport Media via AP Images
(p. 27), Darron Cummings (p. 19), John T. Daniels (p. 23), John J. Gaglielmi/The Courier Times (p. 23), Charles
Krupa (p. 25), Joe Raymond (p. 27), Paul Sancya (p. 21); *Getty Images*: Robert Laberge (p. 21), Francis Miller/
Time Life Pictures (p. 13), B. Anthony Stewart/National Geographic (p. 29); *Glow Images*: © Imagebroker
(p. 26); *iStockphoto*: iStockphoto.com/BasieB (p. 30), iStockphoto.com/benkrut (p. 9), iStockphoto.com/
Davel5957 (p. 9); *Shutterstock*: Joerg Beuge (p. 26), Alena Brozova (p. 30), Steve Byland (p. 30), Kenneth Keifer
(p. 27), Philip Lange (p. 30), Henryk Sadura (p. 5), Alexey Stiop (p. 17), Donald R. Swartz (p. 19).

All population figures taken from the 2010 US census.

Library of Congress Cataloging-in-Publication Data

Murray, Julie, 1969-
   Indiana / Julie Murray.
      p. cm. -- (Explore the United States)
   ISBN 978-1-61783-352-6
   1. Indiana--Juvenile literature. I. Title.
   F526.3.M87 2012
   977.2--dc23
                                  2012004279

Contents

One Nation 4

Indiana Up Close 6

Important Cities 8

Indiana in History 12

Timeline 14

Across the Land 16

Earning a Living 18

Sports Page 20

Hometown Heroes 22

Tour Book 26

A Great State 28

Fast Facts 30

Important Words 31

Web Sites 31

Index 32

ONE NATION

The United States is a **diverse** country. It has farmland, cities, coasts, and mountains. Its people come from many different backgrounds. And, its history covers more than 200 years.

Today the country includes 50 states. Indiana is one of these states. Let's learn more about Indiana and its story!

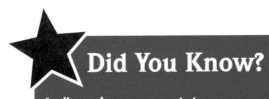

Did You Know?

Indiana became a state on December 11, 1816. It was the nineteenth state to join the nation.

Lake Michigan is on Indiana's northwest border. It is one of the five Great Lakes.

INDIANA UP CLOSE

The United States has four main **regions**. Indiana is in the Midwest.

Indiana has four states on its borders. Michigan is north, and Ohio is east. Kentucky is south, and Illinois is west. Lake Michigan is on Indiana's northwest corner.

Indiana has a total area of 36,417 square miles (94,320 sq km). About 6.5 million people live in the state.

REGIONS OF THE UNITED STATES

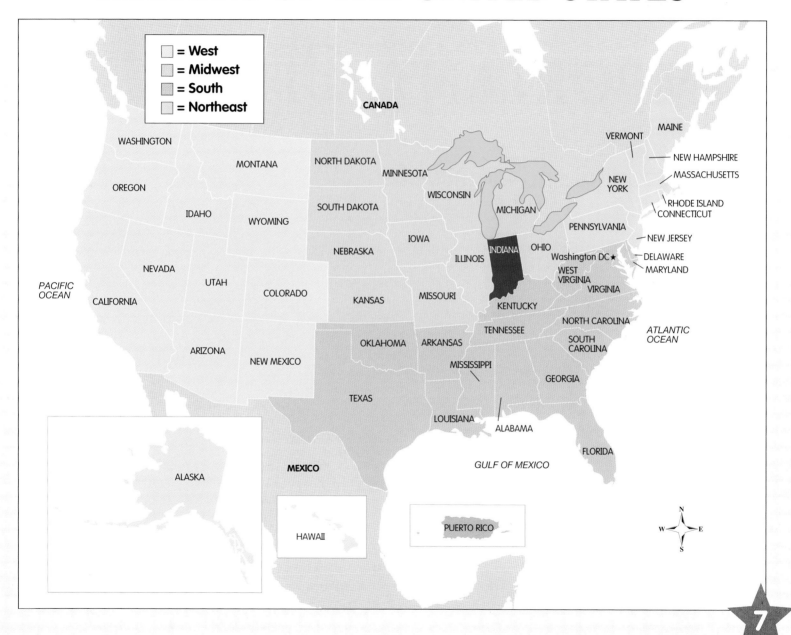

= West
= Midwest
= South
= Northeast

CANADA

WASHINGTON
MONTANA
OREGON
IDAHO
WYOMING
NEVADA
UTAH
CALIFORNIA
COLORADO
ARIZONA
NEW MEXICO

NORTH DAKOTA
MINNESOTA
SOUTH DAKOTA
WISCONSIN
NEBRASKA
IOWA
KANSAS
OKLAHOMA
MISSOURI
ARKANSAS
TEXAS
LOUISIANA

MICHIGAN
ILLINOIS
INDIANA
OHIO
KENTUCKY
TENNESSEE
MISSISSIPPI
ALABAMA
GEORGIA
FLORIDA

VERMONT
MAINE
NEW HAMPSHIRE
MASSACHUSETTS
NEW YORK
RHODE ISLAND
CONNECTICUT
PENNSYLVANIA
NEW JERSEY
Washington DC ★
DELAWARE
MARYLAND
WEST VIRGINIA
VIRGINIA
NORTH CAROLINA
SOUTH CAROLINA

PACIFIC OCEAN
ATLANTIC OCEAN

ALASKA
MEXICO
HAWAII
PUERTO RICO
GULF OF MEXICO

N
W E
S

7

Important Cities

The **capital** and largest city of Indiana is Indianapolis. It is home to 820,445 people. It is called "the Circle City" because of its layout.

The city hosts important sports events. Cars race at Indianapolis Motor Speedway. And, the Indianapolis Colts play football at Lucas Oil Stadium. In 2012, the stadium hosted the Super Bowl for the first time!

A monument in the center of Indianapolis honors war heroes.

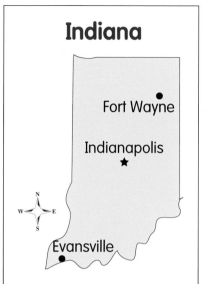

Indiana

Fort Wayne

Indianapolis

Evansville

Lucas Oil Stadium opened in 2008.

Fort Wayne is the second-largest city in Indiana. It has 253,691 people. This city is located where the Saint Marys and Saint Joseph Rivers meet. They join to form the Maumee River.

Indiana's third-largest city is Evansville, with 117,429 people. It is located on the Ohio River. So, it is sometimes called "the River City."

In 2009, Fort Wayne was named an All-American City for the third time. Just ten US cities receive this honor each year!

INDIANA IN HISTORY

Indiana's history includes Native Americans and settlers. Native Americans lived in the area first. In 1679, French explorers arrived by boat. Soon, settlers came to stay. In 1800, the Indiana Territory was created.

In the early years, settlers and Native Americans fought often. After things got more peaceful, Indiana became a state in 1816. In the 1900s, it became known for making steel.

★★★

In the 1900s, Gary was a major steel-producing city.

Timeline

1889

1816

On December 11, Indiana became the nineteenth state.

Standard Oil Company built one of the world's largest refineries in Whiting.

1800s

Past Indiana Territory governor William Henry Harrison became the ninth US president. He died 30 days later.

Elwood Haynes invented one of the first gasoline-powered cars in Kokomo.

1841

1894

1911

The first Indianapolis 500 race took place at Indianapolis Motor Speedway.

1989

Dan Quayle of Indianapolis became vice president of the United States.

2012

Indianapolis hosted the forty-sixth Super Bowl.

1900s

2000s

On December 26, Peyton Manning of the Indianapolis Colts threw his forty-ninth touchdown pass of the season. This broke an NFL record!

2004

ACROSS THE LAND

Indiana has hills, lakes, and rich farmland. Sand **dunes** are found along Lake Michigan. The Wabash River is a major waterway in the state.

Many types of animals make their homes in Indiana. These include raccoons, rabbits, woodchucks, and ducks.

Did You Know?

In Indiana, the average July temperature is 75°F (24°C). In January, it is 28°F (-2°C).

17

EARNING A LIVING

Manufacturing, finance, health care, and **real estate** businesses provide jobs in Indiana. Important products include **chemicals** and automobile parts.

Another important Indiana business is farming. Major crops include corn, soybeans, mint, watermelons, and tomatoes.

Large amounts of **limestone** are found in southern Indiana. The state also mines coal and clay.

New York City's famous Empire State Building (*right*) was built using Indiana limestone (*above*). Some say Indiana limestone is the best in the world.

SPORTS PAGE

Many people think of sports when they think of Indiana. The Indianapolis Colts football team and the Indiana Pacers basketball team both have many fans. College basketball is also very popular!

Indiana is known for car racing, too. The Indianapolis 500, or Indy 500, takes place every year. Top drivers from around the world take part in this famous race.

Sometimes, Indy cars reach 220 miles (354 km) per hour! Even on the freeway, most cars only go about 65 miles (105 km) per hour.

The winning team of the Indy 500 kisses the brick finish line. This practice started in 1996.

Hometown Heroes

Many famous people are from Indiana. Wilbur Wright was born near Millville in 1867. He and his brother Orville are famous inventors. Together, they made the first successful airplane!

On December 17, 1903, Orville flew their airplane near Kitty Hawk, North Carolina. This was the first successful flight. Later that day, Wilbur flew 852 feet (260 m) in about one minute. This was the longest flight on that day.

Orville Wright flew the Wright Flyer for the first time. This plane was powered and could be controlled.

The Wilbur Wright Birthplace and Museum is near Millville.

23

Larry Bird was born in West Baden in 1956. Some say he is one of the greatest basketball players. He became known for having skills in many areas of the game.

Bird played for Indiana State University from 1976 to 1979. He played for the Boston Celtics from 1979 to 1992. After Bird stopped playing, he coached the Indiana Pacers from 1997 to 2000. Today, he has a different job with the team.

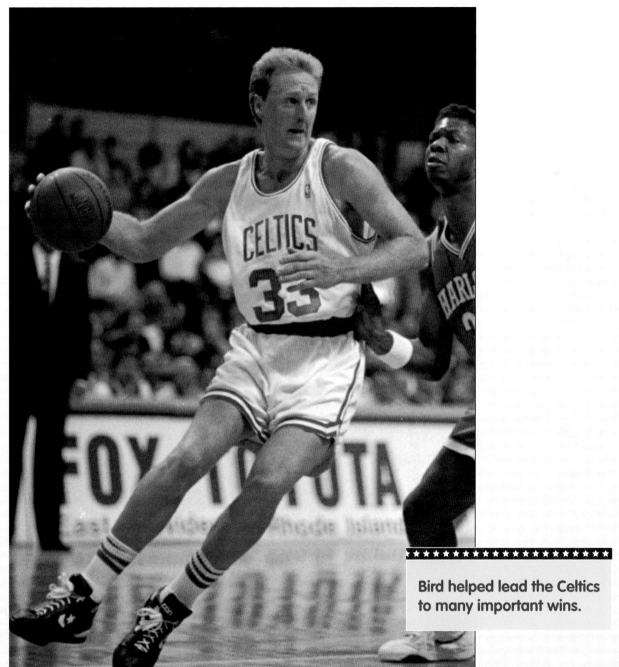

Bird helped lead the Celtics to many important wins.

Tour Book

Do you want to go to Indiana? If you visit the state, here are some places to go and things to do!

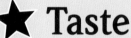 **Taste**

Butter up an ear of corn and enjoy!
Indiana is one of the top US corn growers.

 Listen

Hear some bluegrass music at Indiana's Old Time Music Festival. This event takes place in Metamora on Labor Day weekend. Bluegrass bands often include fiddles, banjos, and mandolins.

★ Learn

Indiana is home to many Amish people. They are known for living simply and free of modern things. Visit Amish Acres in Nappanee to see how they live.

★ Explore

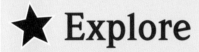

Visit Cataract Falls in Cloverdale. It is the largest waterfall in Indiana!

★ Cheer

Indiana is known for having many basketball fans. Watch an exciting game at Indiana University!

A Great State

The story of Indiana is important to the United States. The people and places that make up this state offer something special to the country. Together with all the states, Indiana helps make the United States great.

Indiana Dunes State Park is located along Lake Michigan. Some of its sand dunes are almost 200 feet (61 m) high!

Fast Facts

Date of Statehood:
December 11, 1816

Population (rank):
6,483,802
(15th most-populated state)

Total Area (rank):
36,417 square miles
(38th largest state)

Motto:
"Crossroads of America"

Nickname:
Hoosier State

State Capital:
Indianapolis

Flag:

Flower: Peony

Postal Abbreviation:
IN

Tree: Tulip Tree

Bird: Northern Cardinal

30

Important Words

capital a city where government leaders meet.

chemical (KEH-mih-kuhl) a substance that can cause reactions and changes.

diverse made up of things that are different from each other.

dune a hill or ridge of loose sand piled up by the wind.

limestone a type of white rock used for building.

real estate the business of selling buildings and land.

region a large part of a country that is different from other parts.

Web Sites

To learn more about Indiana, visit ABDO Publishing Company online. Web sites about Indiana are featured on our Book Links page. These links are routinely monitored and updated to provide the most current information available.

www.abdopublishing.com

Index

Amish Acres **27**

animals **16, 30**

Bird, Larry **24, 25**

businesses **12, 13, 14, 18, 19, 26**

Cataract Falls **27**

Cloverdale **27**

Evansville **10**

Fort Wayne **10, 11**

France **12**

Gary **13**

Harrison, William Henry **14**

Haynes, Elwood **14**

Indiana Dunes State Park **29**

Indianapolis **8, 9, 15, 20, 30**

Indianapolis 500 **15, 20, 21**

Kokomo **14**

Manning, Peyton **15**

Maumee River **10**

Metamora **26**

Michigan, Lake **5, 6, 16, 29**

Midwest (region) **6**

Millville **22, 23**

Nappanee **27**

Native Americans **12**

natural resources **18, 19**

Ohio River **10**

population **6, 8, 10, 30**

Quayle, Dan **15**

Saint Joseph River **10**

Saint Marys River **10**

size **6, 30**

statehood **4, 12, 14, 30**

Wabash River **16, 17**

weather **16**

West Baden **24**

Whiting **14**

Wilbur Wright Birthplace and Museum **23**

Wright brothers **22, 23**